The Soccer Fitness Guide

Mirsad Hasic

DEDICATION

I dedicate this book to my wife.

CONTENTS

Introduction 1
1. The Fundamentals 4
2. Warming Up and Cooling Down 7
   2.1 How to Warm Up – 101 8
      2.1.2 Different Types of Warmup 12
   2.2 The Typical Warmup Routine...13
      2.2.1 Jogging with Exercises (5-15 min) 14
      2.2.2 Dynamic Stretching (5 min)...14
      2.2.3 Light Sprinting (3-5 min) 16
      2.2.4 Static Stretching (5-15 min)..16
   2.3 Cooling Down Routine 18
3. Aerobic & Anaerobic Endurance...21
   3.1 Aerobic Training 22
      3.1.1 Health Benefits of Aerobic Soccer Training: 23
   3.2 Aerobic Specific Exercises...26
      3.2.1 Alternating Jogging and Sprinting.......................................27
      3.2.2 Triangle Runs 28
      3.2.3 Quadrate Runs 29
      3.2.4 Half Field Runs..30
   3.3 Anaerobic Training...31
      3.4 Anaerobic Specific Exercises 32
      3.4.1 Back and Forth...33
      3.4.2 Slalom/Straight Sprints 34
      3.4.3 Fartlek..35
      3.4.4 Sprint & Jog..36
      3.4.5 Pain/Killer Shuttles 37
4. Strength & Power...39
   4.1 Soccer Strength 40
   4.2 Strength Types...42
   4.3 Strength Phases 44
5. Soccer Strength Programs...46
   5.1 Novice...47
      5.1.1 Standing Calf Raises 47
      5.1.2 Calf Press..48
      5.1.3 Back Extensions..50
      5.1.4 Prone Bridge 51
      5.1.5 Triceps Bench Dips 52
      5.1.6 Sit Ups...53
   5.2 Intermediate..54
      5.2.1 Upright Barbell Row...55
      5.2.2 Lunges 56

5.2.3 Seated Leg Press..57
5.2.4 Dumbbell Shoulder Press 58
5.2.5 Step Ups 60
5.2.6 Push Ups 61
5.2.7 Dumbbell Toe Raises 63
5.3 Advanced 64
5.3.1 Seated Cable Row 65
5.3.2 Squats..66
5.3.3 Bench Press 67
5.3.4 Bent Over Row 68
5.3.5 Pull Ups 69
5.3.6 Leg Curls 70
6. Explosive Soccer Power 71
6.1 Plyometric Training is the Way to Go...........................73
6.1.1 Chest Throw With a Sandbag 75
6.1.2 Overhead Throw 76
6.1.3 Pullover Throw 77
6.1.4 Shot Put 78
6.2 Lower Body Plyometric Exercises 79
6.2.1 Bounding...79
6.2.2 Depth Jumps 80
6.2.3 Hurdle Jumps 81
6.2.4 Lateral Jump to Bench/Box....................................82
6.2.5 Ricochets..83
6.2.6 Single Leg Hops 84
6.2.7 Tuck Jumps 85
7. Speed & Agility 86
7.1 Specific Speed for Soccer..87
7.2 Mistakes to Avoid 88
7.3 Speed Exercises 91
7.3.1 Speed Improver..92
7.3.2 Stepping Strides 93
7.3.3 Number Runs 94
7.3.4 Back and Forward...95
7.3.5 Manchester United..95
7.4 Agility Exercises...96
7.4.1 Twenty Yard Box 98
7.4.2 Slalom Runs 99
7.4.3 Station Runs...100
7.4.4 Lateral Double 101
7.4.5 Left-Right Step Ladder..102
7.4.6 In-Out Ladder...103
8 Flexibility Training 96
8.1 Static, Dynamic & Passive Flexibility............................98
8.1.1 Dynamic Flexibility..98

8.1.2 Static Passive Flexibility 99
8.1.3 Static Active Flexibility 99
8.2 Types of Stretching 100
    8.2.1 Static 100
    8.2.2 Dynamic 101
    8.2.3 Ballistic..102
    8.2.4 Proprioceptive neuromuscular facilitation (PNF)...........103
    8.2.5 Isometric..104
8.3 Static Stretching Exercises 105
    8.3.1 Chest 106
    8.3.2 Triceps 107
    8.3.3 Knees to The Chest 108
    8.3.4 Glute Stretch 109
    8.3.5 Groin 110
    8.3.6 Addcut..111
    8.3.7 Single Leg Hamstring..112
    8.3.8 Quadriceps...113
    8.3.9 Standing Calf 114
8.4 Dynamic Stretching 115
    8.4.1 Shifting Stretch 115
    8.4.2 Walking Lunges 116
    8.4.3 Bending at The Sides 117
    8.4.4 Circles 118
    8.4.5 Carioca...119
    8.4.6 High Legs 120
    8.4.7 High Knees..121
9. Programs 122
9.1 Conditioning Program 122
    9.1.1 Week 1 123
    9.1.2 Week 2 123
    9.1.3 Week 3 124
    9.1.4 Week 4 124
    9.1.5 Week 5 125
9.2 Weight Training Program...125
    9.2.1 Legs 126
    9.2.2 Triceps 126
    9.2.3 Back 126
    9.2.4 Core 126
Ending… 127

ACKNOWLEDGMENTS

I would like to thank my family for their support.

Introduction

Without proper fitness training you will never be able to perform at your optimal level on the field.

This might read as an obvious statement but so many amateur players don't quite grasp the concept of "proper fitness training," hence the need for this book.

You may well be a wizard with your ball skills, but none of that really matters if you get worn out halfway through a duel, or simply lack the stamina to sustain your performance for the duration of a game.

Being fit is fundamental for anyone who wants to be a serious player. Fitness is also something which is closely monitored by talent scouts whenever a player catches their eye.

When you are in good physical shape, it is easier for your muscles to coordinate with your nervous system and vice versa, which is yet another good reason to take your fitness seriously. We all know that fitness training can sometimes be quite boring, discouraging even, for those who find it hard to keep up with the drills. But without it there is no you, at least not in the world of competitive soccer there isn't.

Only when you embrace fitness and look at it for what it is - which is a crucial part of being a great soccer player - will you then be able to willingly give 100% focus and effort into the importance of developing in this area.

As well as having that extra-edge performance-wise, a player who is fit and healthy will dramatically reduce his risk of hurt and injury too. It was not until I injured my left knee that I realized the importance of soccer fitness.

Like most other players, I was aware that stretching exercise and other pre-game warm-up techniques were great for preventing injuries, but knowing something without doing anything about it makes that knowledge worthless.

It's all too easy to skip, or not put in the required effort, when it comes to fitness training and warmup exercises, but just know this: those who do take it seriously are much more likely to become seriously competitive players. Those who don't won't.

My first ever serious injury came about because I didn't take fitness seriously at the time.

It actually put me out of action for several months as I went through a long and incredibly boring rehabilitation process.

It was very annoying and frustrating because in this particular case it could have been so easily avoided. In other words, it didn't have to happen. It was during those long months of rehab that I decided to look into injury prevention.

I was keen to learn what things I could be doing to take better care of myself to reduce the risk of injuries and the subsequent hurt and setbacks that is caused by them.

I don't know why it is, but so many young people, including me at the time of my injury, cherry-pick what advice we want to hear from those older, wiser, and more experienced in the sport than we are.

And then we discard anything we're not interested in hearing, despite it being of huge importance. There is this

"I'm indestructible" mindset, and it only wakes up to reality whenever something goes wrong, as something invariably will do with players who don't follow the standard protocol for health and fitness training.

If you want to become a great soccer player and not just settle for being a reasonably good player, then it's time to take total control of your own health, fitness, pre-game warm-up and post-game cooling down regime, and then integrate this into your overall development routine.

Follow the suggestions and tips outlined in my book and I can guarantee you will change the way you think about health and fitness forever.

Not only will you start to feel really great, both physically and mentally, but you will see a marked improvement in the way you perform on the field too.

1. The Fundamentals

In order to strengthen your body for the rigors of a long, hard soccer season, you will need to practice a fitness regime which considers the following six principles:

1. *Strength and endurance*: By ensuring your muscles are strong and resilient you will add extra power to your game and give yourself the staying power you need to play consistently.

2. *Cardiovascular training*: By optimizing your cardiovascular system through regular exercise, your body will be able to convert oxygen into energy more efficiently, which in turn will prevent you from tiring during games.

3. *Fitness and health*: Being fit is one thing but maintaining good health is fundamental so that you can do the training necessary to become fit and stay that way. Being healthy starts by eating well. In other words, you need to be mindful of what foods you can eat and which to avoid. Adapting your diet is something that most of you will need to do if you're serious about enhancing your soccer performance. This means you might need to sacrifice certain types of foods that you have got used to enjoying.

4. *Cutting out unhealthy lifestyle choices*: Most of us have a few unhealthy habits, junk food being one of them, smoking and drinking are two others. You will have to look closely at your lifestyle choices, and if necessary, you will need to make some adjustments to the way you live in order to stay healthy and boost your fitness levels.

5. *The exercise regime*: This will need to be diverse and strict. You must work on all the important areas of fitness in a systematic and complementary fashion.

6. *Understand how your body works*: Getting educated on the workings of your body will surely help you to embrace your health and fitness regime with a renewed enthusiasm. Knowing what happens to your body when you do something, be that a physical exercise or the consumption of certain foods, for example, makes embracing a new health and fitness regime so much easier.

Because of the physical nature of soccer, injuries are always going to be an inevitable part of the game.

Nonetheless, a carefully planned fitness program will contribute toward the prevention of certain injuries, but that's not all it will contribute to.

Being healthy and in good physical shape also means that many injuries will heal quicker when compared to the healing times of those who are not in such good physical shape.

I will discuss the subject of injuries in some depth later in the book, giving advice on how best to tailor your fitness program to suit your own individual fitness needs.

2. Warming Up and Cooling Down

Warming-up is essential for any kind of sport or physical activity, and especially soccer.

You can look at warming-up as something which prepares your body for the forthcoming physical activity by gently informing it that it needs to 'start its engine' in preparation of what's to come.

In more technical terms, a good warm-up increases the movement of blood through your body tissues, thus making your muscles more pliable and therefore less susceptible to injury.

Warming up also increases the delivery of oxygen and nutrients to your muscles. This optimizes them for the physical challenges ahead.

Remember the three quick points below and you will be a lot more enthusiastic about future warm-ups:

1. Warming up decreases the risk of injury.
2. Warming up increases agility, power and overall performance.
3. Warming up mentally prepares and focuses the mind for an upcoming game or practice session.

2.1 How to Warm Up – 101

Many people believe that warming-up simply involves the bending and stretching of muscles.

Although stretching should be a fundamental part of any warm-up routine, other aspects also need to be included, things like jogging, quick sprints, and jumping.

A warmup should always begin slowly and gradually become more intense. This way, your body has time to adapt to each level of increased intensity.

A typical warmup procedure will begin first with some gentle jogging, followed by a quick sprint, followed by yet more jogging.

This process will be repeated several times as a way to get your muscles warmed up and moving.

This warmup exercise also gets your cardiovascular system, or circulatory system, working efficiently by increasing the rate at which blood circulates through the body.

This initial warmup ideally lasts for somewhere between 5-10 minutes. You can adjust the amount of time spent on it according to other factors such as the temperature.

So if it's a hot day you can do less, and if it's a cold day you can do more.

How much time is spent on any particular warmup exercise will also depend on what other exercises are planed into the session.

Once the jogging and sprinting exercise is over, it's time to launch into a stretching routine. A soccer warmup typically consists of three core types of stretching, as follows:

1. Static.
2. Dynamic.
3. PNF stretching (proprioceptive neuromuscular facilitation).

OK, let's now look at each of these in a little more detail, starting with static stretching.

A static stretch simply refers to any stretch that is performed while in a stationary position. It involves holding yourself in a stretched-position for a period of between 15-25 seconds.

While holding your stretch try not to overstretch or flex your muscles. A slight feeling of pain or discomfort is to be expected and quite normal.

Obviously if any stretching exercise becomes too painful or too uncomfortable to withstand, then you are pushing yourself too hard and need to relax the hold.

It's best to start performing static stretches on your ankle and leg muscles first, and then proceed to work systematically up the body in the order described below:

- Calves
- Hamstrings
- Thighs
- Groin
- Hips
- Lower-back
- Shoulders
- Neck

After you have performed all your static stretches it's time to move on to some dynamic exercises.

Dynamic stretches help to prepare your body for the movements typically made during a soccer game.

These will include such things as swinging your legs and twisting your body, the latter of which prepares you for changing direction quickly on the field.

Most dynamic stretches can be performed alone, although some will require a teammate to lean on. In the absence of a teammate, you can simply improvise by using a post or a wall for support.

After a full and comprehensive dynamic-stretch routine, it's time to move on to your final set of stretching exercises known as PNF stretches, or proprioceptive neuromuscular facilitation.

PNF stretches are done to gain extra flexibility in those areas that really do need to be super flexible.

PNF stretches are often used in warm-up routines which are tailored for gymnasts or acrobats.

For a soccer player, PNF stretches give his body that extra bit of agility, thus enabling him to perform a little more robustly.

PNF stretches are also quite intense and should be performed with caution. If you are under the age of 18 then you should not attempt PNF stretches.

The reason for this is because there's is an increased risk of injury for bodies that are still developing.

Make sure that your warm-up routine incorporates all parts of your body, paying special attention to those muscles and actions which are most associated to a typical game of soccer.

In a nutshell, warming up is an essential practice that occurs before any game or practice session.

We warm up because it reduces our risk of injury and it also enables us to play at our optimal level.

That's it.

2.1.2 Different Types of Warmup

The warmup routines outlined above consist of 'general' and 'specific' exercises. There are actually three different categories of warmup routines which I have outlined below:

- *The Passive Warm-up*: A 'passive' warmup is any kind of warmup that does not-involve physical activity. Examples of passive warmup methods include hot showers, steam baths, and massages. In my experience, the most favored of all the passive warmups for soccer players is the massage. The financial implications of hiring a masseuse exclude this as an option for most amateur clubs, but in professional-soccer they are considered essential, and therefore become the norm. If your team can afford a masseuse, then get one. There is no better feeling than having a massage in preparation for a game. After a good massage you will feel in tip-top condition and raring to go.
- *The General Warm-up*: A 'general' warmup is designed to increase your overall body temperature and to wake-up your muscles and joints. A general warmup involves moving and stretching all parts of the body. Unlike a passive warmup, a general warmup consists of actual physical activity, typically jogging and stretching. General warmups are the most common type of warmup practiced in sport prior to a competition or training session.

- *The Specific Warmup*: A specific warmup involves stretching and moving the muscles of your body that will be most used during an upcoming activity, for example, stretching your legs to prepare for running and shooting. Specific warmups are particularly useful if you have recently recovered from an injury and wish to strengthen the part(s) of your body that was injured. Specific warmups are very important, but they are also the type of warmup routine that players tend to neglect the most whenever they get the chance. Remember to focus properly on each of the warmup routines as they are all effective for increasing your performance levels and decreasing the potential for injury.

2.2 The Typical Warmup Routine

In most cases you will warm-up in a group alongside your other teammates.

These warmup sessions are typically controlled by the coach or a teammate who has been designated to take charge.

If you are warming up alone, for whatever reason, then you need to be more disciplined and make sure you don't cut corners by skipping essential exercises.

If you do, then you have an increased risk of injury. Furthermore, you won't perform as well if you fail to follow through with all your warm-up exercises. This is something which is especially evident at the start of a game.

I have created a warmup routine that I use when practicing alone or with a friend, but it can just as easily be used for a team warmup session as well.

Getting into a familiar warmup routine makes it much easier to follow through with than one which is less structured.

2.2.1 Jogging with Exercises (5-15 min)

This type of warmup exercise may vary anywhere from 5-15 minutes. I personally prefer to jog for 10 minutes (at least) in order to wake-up muscles properly and build focus.

2.2.2 Dynamic Stretching (5 min)

Try to incorporate the following dynamic stretching movements into your jog:

- *High Knees*: Hoist your knees up and drive them down in an exaggerated running motion.
- *Butt Kicks*: Kick your heels up behind your back so that they touch, or almost touch, your posterior.

- *High Knee Skipping*: Break into a skip, making sure to raise your knees as high as you can in the process.
- *Power Skipping*: Perform a high-tempo skip whilst ensuring you raise your knees as high as possible in the process.
- *Toe Touch*: Stop jogging briefly and balance on one leg. Now bend down and touch the toes of your grounded foot with the opposite hand, i.e. if your left foot is on the ground use your right hand.
- *Reverse Lunge (with twist)*: Starting off in the standing position, step backwards and lunge with the left foot contacting the left glute muscles. Next, twist over the front leg while moving the left elbow to the outside of the right knee. Now reverse the twist back to neutral position and return to the starting position.
- *Straight Leg March*: While keeping your leg absolutely straight, swing it forward and up to hip level or above. At the height of your leg's movement, touch it with an outstretched hand. Continue the action on both sides as you march forward.
- *Walking Bent Knee Hip*: Bend your knee and move your leg into your body. Finish the move by raising your knee as high as possible.

2.2.3 Light Sprinting (3-5 min)

After I have completed my jogging warmup, along with some of the supplementary exercises, I then proceed with some light runs.

To perform these runs I place two cones in a straight line with a distance of about ten yards between them.

I then run between the cones at approximately 70% of my maximum running potential, taking short intervals of rest (2-3 seconds) upon reaching each cone.

I would typically perform 10 runs in this warm-up routine.

2.2.4 Static Stretching (5-15 min)

Static stretching involves moving into various poses and holding them for a given length of time. This part of your routine should last between 5-15 minutes.

Ideally, try to allow at least 10 minutes for your static stretching exercises if you can as this will allow you enough time to stretch all the necessary muscles.

Most commonly used static stretches include:

- *The Straddle*: Sit down and position your feet so that they are a little more than hip-width apart. Now bend down while keeping your head aligned with your spine. First stretch your arms out and then downward until you touch the toes of your left foot. Now move across and touch your right foot in the same way. Complete the move by then touching the space on the ground between your feet. Repeat the exercise for the required number of repetitions.
- *Standing Groin Stretch*: Start the exercise by standing with your feet wide apart and knees straight. Now bend the right knee out to the side leaning to the right as you go. Hold for between 10-30 seconds depending on ability. Repeat number of repetitions as required.
- *Saigon Squat*: Stand upright with your feet apart at shoulder width and your toes pointing out at about 45 degrees. Keep your back straight and your feet flat as you squat down as low as possible. Use your elbows to push on the inside of the quadriceps and hold the position for a few seconds. Repeat number of repetitions as required.
- *Pretzel Stretch*: Start by lying flat on your back with both knees bent. Next cross one leg over the other so that your foot touches the opposite knee. Now bring both knees toward your chest while gently pulling the uncrossed leg toward you. Stop pulling as soon as you feel a stretch in your buttock. Repeat number of repetitions as required.

- *Standing Quad Stretch*: Start the exercise by standing on your left foot. Now grab your right shin and pull it behind you. Next, tuck your pelvis in as you pull the shin towards your glutes. Once your knee is pointing directly at the ground hold the position for 30 seconds, or less depending on ability. Repeat repetitions on both sides as required.
- *Calf Stretch*: Start this exercise from the push-up position. Now walk your feet towards the hands until your hips are raised. Once your legs are straight and your feet are flat on the ground, place one foot on the back of the other foot, at the ankle. Once you feel a stretching in the calf muscle hold the position for a few seconds. Repeat repetitions on both sides as required.

2.3 Cooling Down Routine

I know from experience that once the coach blows that final whistle you will rarely see anyone going through any cooling-down routines.

Instead, most players proceed straight to the changing rooms and get cleaned up before heading back home, and a few others might hang around to casually practice their free kicks, penalty kicks, or whatever else they fancy doing.

These are all bad habits, and if your coach doesn't care either way what you do after a game or practice session, then you might want to make him aware of the importance of the cooling-down routine.

Cooling-down exercises also reduce the amount of lactic acid in your muscles (too much lactic acid hanging around after a strenuous game can later cause muscle aches and soreness).

And finally, doing cooling-down exercises after any prolonged spells of vigorous activity helps to lower your heart rate and blood pressure.

After a cool-down your body becomes more relaxed as it returns to its more normal, pre-game state.

Try to make the cooling down routine as important to you as the warmup is, and make it an integral part of your overall fitness regime.

It's neither difficult nor time consuming to cool down after vigorous, physical activity, and that makes it one of those rare undertakings where you get out more than you actually put in.

OK, below is a sample cooling-down routine that you can easily follow after your games and practice sessions.

These simple exercises will surely help your body transition to a more restful state:

- *Jog*: The first thing I do when the practice is over is to jog two to three times around the field. Don't cheat on this by cutting on the distance. This is not a race, so take your time and just enjoy the unhurried pace of your jog as you begin to wind down.
- *Walk and Shake*: Walk along the side of the field shaking your arms and legs as you go.

- *Skip and Shake*: As the name suggests, simply skip and shake your arms and legs as you move.
- *Butt Kicks*: Don't perform these with same intensity as you would during a warm-up. When cooling down you need to 'gently' kick your heels to your buttocks using a controlled and unhurried motion.
- *Slow shuffle*: Shuffle in a slow and controlled fashion while keeping your body relaxed.
- *Backward skip*: Skip backwards, again, in a slow and controlled style, making sure to keep your legs and upper body completely relaxed.
- *Static stretching*: Spend a few minutes doing some static stretching (a crucial part of the cooling-down routine).

That's about it.

The above cooling down routine might seem a little intense on the first read, but once you get into a routine, momentum will then kick in and you'll be done in no time at all.

3. Aerobic & Anaerobic Endurance

Different types of exercise are typically classed into two main categories, namely aerobic and anaerobic.

Anaerobic exercise is the shorter-lasting, high-intensity strength-based type of exercise, such as heavy weight-lifting, short sprints and jumping, as three examples.

The fundamental difference between these two forms of exercise is in the way they produce different durations and intensities of muscular contraction, and also by the different ways in which they generate energy in the muscles.

Aerobic training prompts your body to metabolize its fat levels.

Fat metabolism will help you get leaner but could ultimately cause a decline in your performance levels when not managed properly (a phenomenon described in athletic circles as 'hitting the wall').

Anaerobic training converts glycerin, also called glycerol (a type of sugar alcohol found in the body) as its source of energy.

The mode of energy-production induced by anaerobic activity is less efficient than that of aerobic exercise.

3.1 Aerobic Training

As a soccer player, aerobic training is extremely important for your development. It helps to increase your overall stamina which enables you to perform at your very best for the duration of a game without tiring too much.

Scientific studies have clearly shown how players with a high level of aerobic fitness tend to score more goals during the final stages of a soccer game than players who are less fit; the latter group being pretty worn out by the end of an intense competition and therefore less capable.

An increased goal-scoring ability is not the only advantage to be gained from those who maintain peak aerobic fitness-levels.

The list below details a whole host of other benefits that have shown to come about from aerobic training.

3.1.1 Health Benefits of Aerobic Soccer Training:

- Easier to maintain body-weight.
- Lowers blood pressure.
- Decreased heart-rate during periods of both exercise and rest.
- An increased lactic threshold, which helps you to perform better for longer.
- Increased levels of 'good' HDL cholesterol, which help the body to fend off the harmful effects of 'bad' LDL cholesterol.
- An improved ability to tolerate glucose and a reduced resistance to insulin.

As you can see, the potential benefits of aerobic exercise are many.

The most important aspect to any type of exercise though, is to first understand how to perform it correctly.

Therefore, I will begin by illustrating some of the things you should NOT do when performing aerobic exercise.

A lot of people assume that running or jogging long distances over a prolonged period of time will help them attune their aerobic fitness to the demands of their soccer career.

This is not actually the case.

Running long distances on a regular basis will indeed see your muscles adapt to a long and slow form of aerobic activity, but this is unsuited to the high-tempo, short-bursts of activity required in the game of soccer.

Running long-distances definitely hardens an athlete for the long slog of a marathon, but it actually decreases the ability of a soccer player to perform short, sharp bursts of physical activity such as sprinting, turning quickly to change direction, jumping, and so on, all of which are essential to the game.

So let us look at how you should practice aerobic activity in a way that will actually enhance your soccer performance on the field.

I will start by introducing one extremely effective method for developing your aerobic soccer fitness using tempo-runs.

Tempo runs require that you perform short bursts of intense aerobic sprints, similar to what will be performed on the field.

This type of exercise, therefore, focuses specifically on all the right areas.

Although simple in approach, there are a few things required in order to make sure tempo runs are practiced to their best effect.

- As you run, make sure you keep your arms loose and relaxed.
- The upper-half of your body should be leaning slightly forward in order to avoid injury and to maximize your running style.
- Muscles need to be relaxed and straight, meaning you mustn't deliberately tense your body up.
- Try to keep your body stable and balanced.
- Run with large strides to quicken the pace as much as possible.

As I run I try to focus on the importance of remaining relaxed while leaning slightly forward using proper arm movements.

By doing this I am able to achieve optimal speed and balance.

Because tempo runs don't last long, this lets me run as fast as I possibly can knowing that the sprint will quickly come to an end.

I regard these as the three most basic and essential rules of running, and by adhering to them I have been able to increase and maintain good speed and acceleration when playing soccer.

Running exercise is not complicated but it is physically demanding, and it also takes prolonged practice and focus before you can reach the required levels of speed and fitness.

Like any other form or training, patience and persistence will get you to where you need to be.

So by keeping up with your fitness routine you will find that your fitness and performance levels will not only improve dramatically but you will also be able to maintain a constant level of fitness once you reach your peak.

Skipping or skimping on your fitness regime, on the other hand, will have the opposite effect.

3.2 Aerobic Specific Exercises

Higher aerobic endurance will help you to cover more yards more often. This means you'll be able to participate more in your team's offensive game, and also be able to help your side in its defensive efforts as well. Aerobic fitness will enhance your performance box-to-box, and add to your all-round ability.

Having good stamina is of huge importance, especially toward the end of games when energy levels naturally begin to deplete.

The following exercises will help you to enhance your aerobic levels.

3.2.1 Alternating Jogging and Sprinting

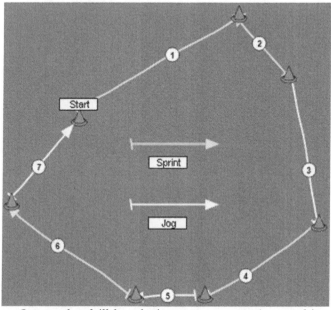

Set up the drill by placing seven cones (or anything else that can be used to mark the points) in the same layout as the illustration below.

As you can see, the exercise alternates between jogs and sprints. Try only to sprint at about 70% of your maximum speed.

The distance between the cones should increase gradually.

This is a conscious strategy to make you work harder as you move around the circuit.

3.2.2 Triangle Runs

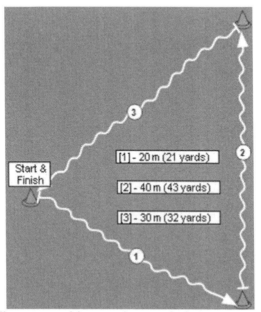

Start &
Finish

[1] - 20 m (21 yards)

[2] - 40 m (43 yards)

[3] - 30 m (32 yards)

I like to use this exercise regularly as a part of my overall aerobic routine.

You can set it up very easily by placing the cones in a triangular formation as in the illustration below. Start at the first cone, running at about 50% of your maximum speed.

Once you reach the second cone increase your speed to 60%, and finish the third leg at 70% of your maximum running speed.

The hardest thing with this drill is to get your speed just right, but with a little practice this is something that will come more naturally to you over time.

Although this drill can be performed on any kind of surface, it will require a lot of space.

If necessary, you can adapt the drill by decreasing the distance between the cones to suit the area available to you.

3.2.3 Quadrate Runs

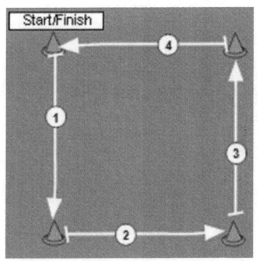

This is a different way to cover the length of a soccer field. Simply place 4 cones approximately 25 meters (27 yards) apart, and start to run at 60% of your maximum speed.

You could vary this exercise by increasing the speed to 70% or shift your speed between the cones (see illustration below).

Examples:

- Distance 1 run at 60%
- Distance 2 run at 70%
- Distance 3 run at 60%
- Distance 4 run at 70%.

You can also run with a soccer ball here and use this exercise as a part of your warm up routine if you want to.

3.2.4 Half Field Runs

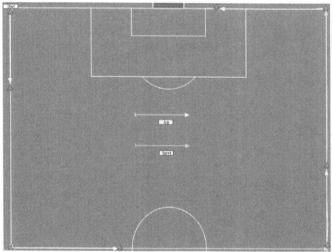

This exercise can be performed with or without cones but it is better to use them if you can because you will be able to orientate yourself easier and also know 'exactly' when to increase your speed.

I have omitted the distance between the cones here because it can vary depending on the length of the field (a field can be anywhere from 90-120m (98-131 yards)).

Whatever size field you practice on, use the image below as a template.

The yellow arrows show when to sprint (keep to about 70% of your maximum speed) and the white ones show when to jog.

Start the drill by jogging downfield from the first cone located at the top left.

3.3 Anaerobic Training

This type of training alternates intervals of intense activity and rest, obviously something which is very applicable to playing soccer.

Anaerobic training is also great for burning calories and decreasing excess body fat.

It is more intense compared to aerobic training but the main difference is that anaerobic training is shorter in duration.

You will often hear anaerobic training being referred to as quality exercise.

Because this form of workout requires a lot of energy, which derives from glycogen within the body, it is therefore crucial to eat the right foods to prepare your body for training.

When performing anaerobic training, lactic acid is produced in your muscles.

This lactic acid can cause fatigue and discomfort if too much build up is allowed.

This is the reason why anaerobic training cannot be performed for long durations.

Anaerobic sprint exercises are usually performed at intervals similar to those below:
- Sprint 20 sec
- Rest 1 min
- Sprint 25 sec
- Rest 1 min and so on...

The main four fitness advantages you will gain as soccer player from anaerobic training are:

1. The ability to change speeds over long distances and with less fatigue.
2. Easier to maintain your top speed.
3. Easier to maintain your soccer ball skills.
4. Ability to maintain your concentration due to the absence of fatigue.

3.4 Anaerobic Specific Exercises

These exercises are very effective when performed properly and with maximum effort.

You should therefore always try to squeeze out the very last drop of energy during your anaerobic training.

Reminder: Don't ever forget to warmup properly before attempting any of the exercises below

3.4.1 Back and Forth

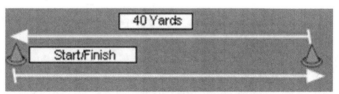

This is a simple yet incredibly effective exercise that doesn't require any specific equipment.

Start at the cone to the left (see illustration below) and perform a run at 70% of your total speed.

Once you reach the second cone, sprint back at the same speed to the starting cone.

Rest for 30-40 seconds and repeat the exercise. Try to perform at least five reps.

Tip: You can also vary this exercise by involving a ball sometimes as it can be an effective way to practice both fitness and ball control at the same time.

3.4.2 Slalom/Straight Sprints

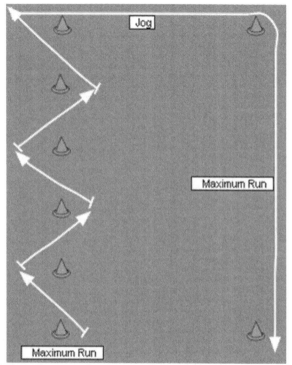

The distance between the cones is optional and depends on how fit you are at the time of workout.

Start from the first cone at the bottom left (see illustration below) and work your way through the cones as indicated by the arrows.

Once you reach the top cone, jog gently over to the seventh cone (top right corner).

Now perform a maximum run to the last cone (bottom right corner) and then walk or jog gently back to the starting position.

One thing you should keep in mind here is to really push yourself during the exercise.

Don't forget too that the more you put in to your training the more you will get out of it.

3.4.3 Fartlek

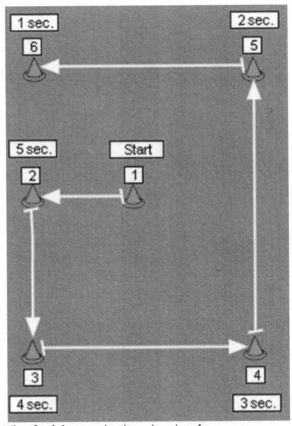

The fartlek exercise is quite simple to set up.

You will need six cones in total and a relatively large area to practice in.

The distance from cone one to cone two should be about 5-10 yards, from cone two to cone three about 10-15 yards, from cone three to cone four about 15-20 yards, from cone four to cone five about 20-25 yards, and from cone five to cone six about 25-30 yards (see illustration below).

3.4.4 Sprint & Jog

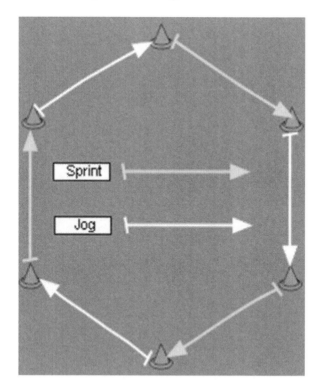

Set up six cones about five yards apart in a set formation (see illustration below).

You may vary this drill by increasing the distance between the cones or by removing the jogging part and running at your maximum for each repetition.

Try to do at least five reps in a row and rest for about 15 seconds between each repetition.

3.4.5 Pain/Killer Shuttles

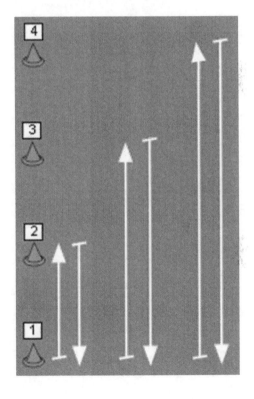

This exercise is ideal for the end of a training session because it will squeeze every last drop of energy out of you when performed with real determination.

OK, place four cones 10-15 yards apart (see illustration below).

Starting at cone one, sprint to cone two and back again to cone one. Now sprint to cone three and back to cone one.

Finally, sprint to cone four and back to cone one.

Try to run at maximum speed when performing this drill.

Make sure to rest for twenty to thirty seconds during each of the repetitions.

Attempt to repeat the exercise five to ten times.

4. Strength & Power

Your ability to shield the ball, shoot harder, and quickly accelerate past opponents, depends on your strength and power.

A soccer player who is not exceptionally strong and doesn't possess an explosive capability will rarely perform well on the field, or certainly not with any continuity, and definitely not towards the end of a game.

If you want to be more than just another average soccer player then you will need to put in lots of effort at improving your overall strength and power.

Of course this is not something that will come overnight and you should be mindful of that fact.

Even so, providing you are determined and resilient in your approach you will get to where you want to be and become that better player you always dreamt of becoming.

4.1 Soccer Strength

The biggest misunderstanding with regards to soccer strength is that many players think that strength building means creating big muscles.

It's not.

Strength training for soccer players should not focus on building physiques but on exercises that are specifically aimed at producing overall strength and endurance in the player.

Furthermore, becoming strong and muscular, as is the case with body building, does not necessarily make a person fit, the latter of which is crucial for anyone who wants to stay the course on a soccer field.

To perform well as a soccer player you need to have good strength in both the lower and the upper body.

Almost every movement on the soccer field, i.e. shooting, sprinting, heading, kicking, and so on, requires a good foundation of strength and power and fitness.

Getting to big and too muscular only slows you down, which kind of defeats your goal if you're hoping to become as fast as you can be.

Let us now look at how strength will actually improve your performance. Below are some of the skills that you will be able to perform much better the more physical strength you have:

- *Shooting Power*: Most of your shooting power is actually generated from the lower back and abs. By focusing on the muscles in these areas you will soon be able to fire harder and longer shots.

- Shielding the Ball: The stronger you are, the harder it will be for your opponents to get a touch on the ball when you're shielding it from them. You will also be able to push your opponents away, without breaking the rules, of course, and create more time and space for yourself to do something useful with the ball.

- *Improved Balance*: Your legs are the key to good balance. It is therefore important to improve the strength in your legs. Having strong legs helps with your dribbling, heading and tackling skills, simply by facilitating better balance.

- *Heading*: Being able to jump high is crucial in order to beat opponents in heading duels. This requires solid strength in both your lower and upper body.

Now that you know why soccer strength is so important, let us move on and take a look at the different types of strength that should be focused on.

4.2 Strength Types

As a soccer player you will need to focus on the three types of strength: max strength, muscle power and muscular or strength endurance.

- *Max Strength*: Good max strength is important for tackling, shielding, and for holding off your opponents. Even more significant is that it forms the foundation of your speed and power. What's important to understand is that in order to achieve maximum strength you need to focus on your abdominals, lower back and trunk, which all form your center of power. Every turn, stop, and start that you perform is supported by your core. Involving max strength training in your overall practice regime will surely increase your performance on the field.

- *Muscle Power*: Your muscle power determines your max strength and the speed of your movement. Increasing one of these, without lowering the other, will enhance your explosive power. Using weights is great for growing your overall muscular power. However, be mindful not to overdo this. Remember, it is an exercise in muscle toning, not body building. Keep in mind that muscles which are too big can actually decrease your flexibility and speed on the field.

- *Muscular or Strength Endurance*: In soccer, muscular endurance is defined as the ability of one or several muscle groups to perform repeated, high intensity movements. Training for your muscular endurance should be performed with light weights and lots of repetitions. One popular method for increasing your strength power is to participate in circuit training (probably the most widely used method for soccer endurance). This is a method where several exercise stations are laid out in a formation from where individual drills are apportioned to each of the stations. Many exercises involved in circuit training don't even need a lot of equipment, if any at all. Such drills include things like pushups, bench-steps, bench dips, crunches, and so on.

4.3 Strength Phases

Breaking your training up into soccer strength phases is an important part of your overall fitness program. In soccer, the four most commonly used strength phases are:

- *The Off-season Phase*: During the off season, you should focus mainly on building your functional strength. The off season phase has two primary goals. The first one is to prepare your body for the pre-season. This may include lifting light weights, playing recreational soccer, jogging and so on. I would recommend that you practice at least twice a week as way of keeping in shape. The other goal is to let your body recover. During the off season phase, you should rest at least two weeks without participating in any physical activities at all. You should just take the time out and enjoy the easy life for a bit. Try also to eat more, but not so much that you start to gain unwanted pounds.

- *Early pre-season*: During the early pre-season you should focus mainly on building your maximum strength. You should try to complete this phase before the start of your first regular season game. This phase should be the most physically demanding so you should really put in big effort here to perform with maximum determination.

- *Late Pre-Season*: In the late pre-season phase your main goal is to convert your strength into muscular endurance. To achieve this you will need to participate in plyometric, or jump training, along with circuit training, rather than weight training. The late pre-season could vary from anywhere between four to eight weeks.
- *In-Season Phase*: If you want to become a well-rounded player you will need to accept the fact that you'll lose some max strength as you develop other skills. However, you should not worry about this too much because it will make you a better player overall, not a worse one. During the in-season phase, your goal is to maintain the fitness levels that you've built up during the pre-season period. You will also need to split your strength training up into several different cycles. Each of these may last for six to seven weeks.

In the first three weeks, you should only lift light weights.

In weeks four and five, you can transition to heavier weights.

During weeks six and seven you should return to lifting lighter weights again.

5. Soccer Strength Programs

The following strength programs are separated into the various skill levels, those being novice, intermediate and advanced.

If you are new to soccer, then I recommend you to begin with the novice program as it is the most basic and therefore the most effective one to get you started.

If you have been playing soccer for a while but feel that you're lacking in strength, then it's a good idea to begin with the intermediate program.

If you are already a well-trained player in good overall shape, but would like to improve your strength somewhat, then you should jump directly into the advanced program.

OK, let's look a little closer at each of these soccer strength programs in more detail.

5.1 Novice

This is a function strength program that should be followed for 8-10 weeks.

There are four important things you need to keep in mind before starting on this program:

1. Always warmup your whole body before attempting any of the exercises.
2. Do not perform any of these exercises more than twice per week.
3. Don't rest more than one minute between each of the exercises.
4. Perform circuit training for two weeks before starting the novice program. This way you will prepare your body for the more physical drills ahead.

5.1.1 Standing Calf Raises

The standing calf raises will strengthen your ankles. This makes you more resistant to various ankle injuries that can occur during a soccer game.

These same ankle exercises can also be a part of your ankle rehabilitation program if you are already injured or suffering from an old injury.

How to perform Standing Calf Raises:

1. Stand in an upright position.
2. Raise your heels as you breathe out by extending your ankles as high as possible while flexing your calf muscles.
3. Slowly lower yourself back down.
4. Repeat repetitions as required.

Tip: Once you get comfortable doing this exercise you could try to vary it by tucking your right foot behind your left heel and vice-versa.

5.1.2 Calf Press

The lower leg muscles are known to be the hardest to develop and strengthen, but don't worry, your local gym will surely have a calf press machine (see illustration below).

This equipment is not hard to use but it's not that obvious either.

Therefore, you might need someone to show you how to operate it if it's your first time.

How to perform the Calf Press:

1. Grasp the handles that are located on either the front or at the side of the machine, depending on the model.
2. Now push the lever upward by extending your ankles as far as possible.
3. Return to the starting position by relaxing your ankles until your calves become stretched.

Tip: Once you complete a set, make sure to stretch your calf muscles for about 25-30 seconds.

Keep your knees straight during the exercise.

5.1.3 Back Extensions

Back extensions are great for strengthening your lats (the largest muscles in the back).

By having stronger and more resistant muscles in your back you will be able to prevent several injuries that are associated with this muscle group.

How to Perform Back Extensions:

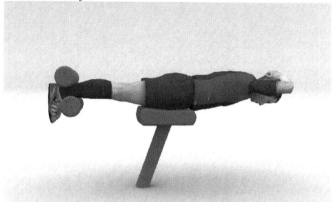

1. Place your hands behind your head and then contract your abs.
2. Start to bend at the waist, up and down, in a slow and controlled motion.
3. Increase the resistance by holding small weight plates behind the neck.

Tip: If you are new to this exercise I suggest you only use your bodyweight as resistance, not the weight plates.

Perform the exercise at a moderate rate and also make sure you keep your legs straight.

5.1.4 Prone Bridge

The prone bridge exercise will not only develop your core strength, it will also improve your stability during other exercises that are performed in a prone (face down) position such as pushups and prone rows.

How to Perform Prone Bridge:

1. Align your toes under your ankles and your forearms under the shoulders.
2. Keep your hips and back flat.
3. Draw your navel toward your spine and then brace your core.
4. Keep your body in a straight line posture hold.

Tip: Try to maintain a straight line from your heels all the way to your head. Try not to let your butt and hips sag or poke upwards.

5.1.5 Triceps Bench Dips

The triceps bench dips develop your entire triceps at the same time as your pectoral muscles. You can do this exercise by either using your body as weight or adding weights in order to increase the resistance.

How to Perform Triceps Bench Drips:

1. Start by placing your hands on the bench behind you and your heels on the bench in front of you.
2. Keep your back straight at all times.
3. Move down slowly while keeping your back close to the bench behind you.
4. Push yourself back up to the starting position.

Tips: Note that the two benches need to be of the same height.

Make sure you don't dip down too low as this will place unnecessary stress on your shoulder joints, which is something that could lead to injury.

Try to squeeze your triceps once you reach the top of the movement in order to gain maximum benefit from this exercise.

5.1.6 Sit Ups

Performing sit-ups is a good way to develop stronger abdominal muscles.

This section of muscles is crucial for plying successful soccer.

You will, for example, be able to win more duels, run faster, and also decrease the risk of getting injured.

How to Perform Sit Ups:

1. Start by lying down on the ground. Keep your knees bent and place your feet flat on the floor.
2. Tighten your abdominal muscles.
3. Lift your upper body about 45 degrees from the ground.
4. Hold that position for a second.
5. Slowly return to your starting position and repeat the action. Try to do at least 30-40 reps per set. If you can't achieve this many, make it a personal goal to aim for.

Tip: Don't pull your head with your hands while performing the exercise.

5.2 Intermediate

As mentioned earlier, the intermediate program is ideal if you have been playing soccer for a while but wish to improve on your overall strength.

Before you begin there are some important things I want you to keep in mind:

- Follow this program for about six to eight weeks.
- Always warm up your entire body before attempting any of these exercises.
- Do not rest more than three minutes between each exercise and try to perform each session in less than 45 minutes.
- Start by performing three sets of 12-15 repetitions per exercise. The last three reps of each set should be the hardest ones. If you barely have any power left at the last rep then you have done well.
- Increase the weight progressively after each week and reduce the number of reps per exercise. However, do not go lower than 10 reps per set.

5.2.1 Upright Barbell Row

The upright barbell row is very useful for the development of your shoulders and the trapezius muscles.

The trapezius muscles are two large triangular muscles that extend along the back of the neck and shoulders.

They're responsible for moving, rotating, and stabilizing the scapula (shoulder blade) and extending the head at the neck and moving the head and shoulder blade.

Although the upright barbell row exercise may seem pretty easy to perform, it still requires a lot of technique and practice before it can be mastered well.

How to Perform Upright Barbell Row:

1. Grasp the barbell and let it hang down in front of you.
2. Keep your body straight and make sure that your hands are in line with your thighs.
3. Lift up the barbell toward your chin.

4. Stop when you get to just below the neck level.
5. Return slowly to the starting position.

Tips: Do not over rotate your arms, as this could lead to an injury. Also, make sure you have the right grip because failure to grip properly could cause stress injuries to the bones of your hands.

5.2.2 Lunges

Lunges are great for strengthening your lower body. They work all your major leg muscles, including the hamstrings, quads and calves.

Lunges are also energy consuming which means you will be able to burn a lot of calories while performing them.

How to Perform Lunges:

- Start by placing your hands behind on your head, pull the shoulders back, and stand tall.
- Step forward with your right leg and slowly lower the body until the front knee is bent to 90 degrees (the back knee should never touch the floor).
- Push yourself back up to the starting position quickly but carefully.
- Repeat with the left leg.

Tips: When bending the knee you should maintain a 90° angle.

Do not go beyond your toes because if you do, you may injure yourself.

Do not set your both legs in a straight line. Instead, try to keep them horizontally separated by about six inches in order to maintain your balance.

If you feel pain in your knee during the exercise, you are probably performing it incorrectly or have an old injury.

Make sure to consult with either a trainer or a medical professional if you have any of these issues.

5.2.3 Seated Leg Press

The main purpose of this exercise is to strengthen the front of your upper legs (the quads) and the back of your lower legs (the calves).

Since the leg press works several of your muscles at once, it makes this a very efficient way to strengthen your lower body.

How to Perform Seated Leg Press:

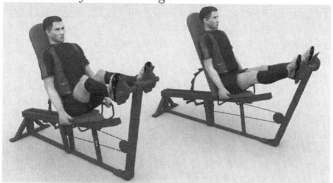

1. Sit down in a comfortable position while keeping your upper body upright.
2. Release the safety mechanism and push the platform up.
3. Lower the platform down as far as possible and try not to put stress on your lower back.

Tips: Keep your knees in line with your feet. Keep your head steady against the supporting pad. Straighten your legs during the resistance.

5.2.4 Dumbbell Shoulder Press

The dumbbell shoulder press is a very efficient exercise for strengthening your shoulders, triceps and forearms.

If you can't lift up the dumbbells in the proper starting position without assistance, then your dumbbells are too heavy.

I would therefore advise you to switch to a lighter pair of dumbbells until you gain more strength.

How to Perform Dumbbell Shoulder Press:

1. Take the dumbbells firmly in each of your hands and sit down on a bench (preferably one with back support).
2. Plant your feet on the ground keeping them hip width apart.
3. Bend your elbows and then raise your upper arms to shoulder height so that the dumbbells are about ear level.
4. Make sure to pull your abdominals in so that there's a slight gap between the bench and your back.
5. Check that the back of your head is resting against the head support.
6. Now, push the dumbbells to ear level, hold the position for one second, and then lift them up above your head.
7. Move them back to the ear level and then repeat the action.

Tips: Avoid arching your back excessively when doing this exercise as it could cause an injury. Don't hold the dumbbells too far in toward your head.

If you were to lose control they could smack down hard on your cranium.

5.2.5 Step Ups

Step-ups are great for developing your thigh muscles. This is one of my favorite exercises for a number of reasons.

How to Perform Step Ups:

1. Stand next to a bench while keeping a barbell behind your head in line with the top of your shoulders.
2. Step onto the bench with one foot and then bring up the other foot so that you are standing on the bench firmly with both feet.

3. Return to the ground by stepping backward off the bench using the same foot that you first stepped onto the bench with, followed by the other foot.

Tip: Don't, at any point, lean your torso forward excessively as you could fall and lose control of the barbell and risk serious injury.

5.2.6 Push Ups

This is one of the most effective exercises for improving your overall soccer fitness.

Although considered boring by some, just know that pushups can be varied in many different ways.

Pushups offer the benefit of weight lifting and stretching in a single exercise.

How to Perform Push Ups:

1. Face down keeping your hands slightly wider than shoulder width apart.
2. Position your feet so that they feel comfortable to you. That might be tight together or some distance apart, whatever works best is fine.

3. The first contact with the ground should be made with your chin and not with your nose, so when you perform your pushup, your head will be looking slightly ahead (looking up also helps to keep your body in line).
4. Push your body up off the floor until your arms are straight and locked.
5. Once you reach the top, hold that position 1-2 seconds and lower your body slowly.
6. Pause for 1-2 seconds and then repeat again for the required repetitions.

Tips: Avoid dropping your head or the lower back.

Also make sure that your hips don't drop too low or rise too high during the pushups.

5.2.7 Dumbbell Toe Raises

The calf muscles help you to walk and run more effectively by allowing you to perform better controlled "push off the ground" movements.

Raised toe exercises are a great way to strengthen and develop this muscle group.

How to Perform Dumbbell Toe Raises:

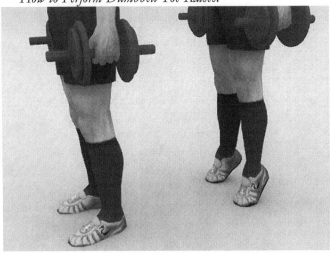

1. Start by standing on the ground with your feet no wider than shoulder width apart.
2. Lift your heels off the ground until you are standing completely on your toes.
3. Try to hold that position for at least three seconds before lowering back down.

Tips: Start with light weights first and work your way up to heavier weights. If you try to use too much weight at the beginning, you could trigger inflammation in the calf muscles.

Keep your body upright and don't bend forwards or backwards while performing this exercise.

5.3 Advanced

Because you are already strong, you should apply some weights that will force you to squeeze out the very last drop of power during the final three reps of each set.

Before you go on, make sure you remember the following important points:

- Always warm up properly and thoroughly before the start of any workout.
- Try not to rest more than three minutes between the exercises. However, if you feel that you need little more time to recover then it is fine to do so until you are able to adapt.
- You should be able to complete this session in around one hour.

5.3.1 Seated Cable Row

This is a great exercise for developing the thickness of your middle back area. This exercise requires a low cable machine. This can usually be found in most well-equipped gyms.

How to Perform Dumbbell Toe Raises:

- Adjust the seat according to your own height.
- Grasp the handles while keeping your arms completely stretched.
- Pull the handles towards you and return slowly to the starting position.

Tip: It is very important to keep your back straight during the whole exercise.

Do not let your shoulders hunch over when you extend your arms.

5.3.2 Squats

The barbell squat is one of the most advanced exercises when it comes to soccer strength drills.

If you place too much weight on the barbell without knowing your strength, you could easily injure yourself, so be extremely careful with this.

Start with light weights first and move your way up as you learn the right technique.

How to Perform Squats:

1. Stand with your legs shoulder width apart and place the barbell on the trapezius muscles.
2. Lower yourself into a squat while having your knees in line with your toes.
3. Once your thighs are at a 90 degree angle, pause momentarily and then return to the starting position.

Tips: Make sure to keep your head forward, back straight, and feet flat on the floor.

Your knees should point in the same direction as your feet during the repetitions.

Never place the barbell directly on your neck as this could lead to very serious injuries.

5.3.3 Bench Press

This is another of my personal favorites as it builds the muscles of the chest as well as the triceps and shoulder muscles.

Another great thing with this exercise is that you can perform it with barbells, dumbbells, or even with a Smith machine (a piece of equipment that looks like a bench press but has guiding rails. These rails keep the barbell in a straight up and down line).

How to Perform Bench Press:

1. Lie down on the bench and make sure the barbell is at a comfortable height.
2. Bring the barbell carefully out of its rest and lower it slowly to your chest.
3. Once it slightly touches your chest, push the barbell back into place while keeping your butt on the bench and feet steady on the ground.

Tips: Do not keep the barbell too high as it will be hard to rack it. Make sure you keep your feet firmly on the floor during the whole repetition. Do not bring your butt off the bench (one of the most common mistakes when performing the bench press).

5.3.4 Bent Over Row

The bent over row is ideal for developing the posterior part of the deltoid in your shoulder.

Many soccer players tend to focus only on the muscles at the front of their shoulders.

This exercise will help you avoid that by giving you a more balanced muscle development.

How to Perform Bent Over Row:

1. Stand with your feet apart and knees slightly bent. Place one of your hands on the bench so that your upper body is parallel to the ground.
2. Hold a dumbbell while keeping your arm perpendicular to the ground.
3. Squeeze your shoulder blades and pull the dumbbell toward you while keeping your elbow as high as possible.
4. Return to the starting position and repeat the action.

Tip: Make sure to keep your torso straight and your elbows close to your body during the repetitions.

5.3.5 Pull Ups

This is one of the best but also hardest exercises that you can do for building your upper body, back, and core strength.

The exercise does not require any advanced equipment which makes it ideal for days when you can't get to the gym.

How to Perform Pull Ups:

1. Grab the bar with an overhand grip.
2. Allow your body to hang in the air while keeping it relaxed.
3. Pull yourself up and then immediately return to the starting position once you pass the bar with your chest.

Tips: Stand on a bench before pulling yourself up in order to avoid a build-up of lactic acid. You could use a weight vest in order to increase the resistance.

5.3.6 Leg Curls

Leg curls are great for strengthening your hamstrings, the muscles located along the rear of your thighs.

These muscles are responsible for bending the knees and accelerating.

By developing them you will be able to run longer distances and therefore decrease your fatigue during games.

How to Perform Leg Curls:

-   Lie face down on the bench.
-   Adjust the bar so that it feels comfortable around your ankles.
-   Grasp the supporting handles and then lift the rear bar upward as you flex your knee joints.
-   Pull the bar back far enough so that it touches your buttocks.
-   Lower the bar back slightly and then repeat the movement.

Tips: Perform the exercise slowly and concentrate on the moves as you do them.

You will need to stretch your hamstrings between the sets. The up motion needs to be a little faster than the down motion.

6. Explosive Soccer Power

You know by now that having good overall strength is crucial for playing great soccer.

However, knowing something without doing anything with that knowledge means nothing.

Understanding how to convert this power into explosive energy is the key for using it to great effect. That is what this chapter is all about.

Imagine that you have such great strength that very few opponents ever get to win a heading duel against you.

You are also superior at shielding the ball, and opponents who attempt to get at it just bounce off you like flies trying to enter through a closed window.

Sounds good, right?

But now let's look at other scenario. Let's say you can't win any rebounds because you are just a bit too slow in the first five to ten yards.

You can't get around your opponents in one on one dribbling duels either because your opponents always seem to be that much quicker on their feet than you are.

Furthermore, you have a hard time marking your opponents because they are constantly moving, thus making your life on the field exhausting and frustrating.

All of a sudden you realize that you strength is only taking you so far.

And because of your lack of explosive power, this is making you fail in so many other important areas of the game.

Now you may be thinking: *Wait a minute, why not just start practicing on my power and just skip the strength training part?*

You would not be the first person to think like this, but whatever you do don't let your thinking convince you that power without strength is a good idea, because it's not.

It's akin to trying to drive a car without any fuel. In short, you need strength because it converts your energy into power, or to put it another way, physical strength is the driving force behind your power.

The main purpose of the exercises in the strength part of this chapter is to lay a fundamental base for your explosive power training.

Without them, you are falling short.

There are various ways that you can improve your explosive power.

In fact, there will probably be as many suggestions as there are people you ask.

However, my personal favorite, which is also the most popular for many professional players, uses a method called plyometric training; something we are going to look at next.

6.1 Plyometric Training is the Way to Go

Plyometric training, also known as "jump training" or "plyos," is made up of explosive exercises that create stretch reflexes in your muscles, thus exerting maximum force in short intervals of time.

The biggest danger with this type of training is that you can cause yourself several injuries if you don't have a fundamental strength base before you start out.

Believe it or not, but many coaches of amateur teams are not always aware of this fact.

They quite often put their players on an intensive plyometric program and then wonder why so many complain about hurt and injury soon after.

I've actually experienced this 'lack of understanding' with a few of my old coaches in my earlier days of playing amateur soccer.

In almost all of the cases where someone ended up hurt, the coaches would blame the players for not following the routines properly.

Alas, this ignorance and the consequent injuries continue to this day, unfortunately.

OK, so based on the above, it is crucial for you to take responsibility for any plyometric training that you do.

In order to do these drills safely and effectively you will need to have an understanding on what happens to your muscles during the exercises.

When doing plyometric exercise, your muscles go from an eccentric (lengthened) position to a concentric (shortened) position, and then back to a resting position, all within a short space of time.

Your nervous system is highly switched on during these actions.

You can say that the main objective of your plyometric training is to reduce your contact time with the ground as you sprint, jump or kick, depending on the exercise being performed.

Before you begin on any plyometric exercise regime I want you to understand that you really do need to have a solid strength foundation in place.

As mentioned earlier, having the necessary strength is not only crucial if these exercises are to improve your explosive power, but it also helps to reduce the possibility of injury.

Moreover, these exercises will allow you to advance onto more intense variations of plyometric training as you develop further into your program.

OK, on that note let's begin to look at some of the most effective plyometric exercises for boosting your explosive power on the field.

6.1.1 Chest Throw With a Sandbag

How to Perform Chest Throw With a Sandbag:

- Stand facing into free space.
- Your feet should be no wider than shoulder width apart.
- Lift the sand bag with your arms and hold it at chest level.
- Push it out (throw it) in front of you with as much explosive power as you can muster.

6.1.2 Overhead Throw

How to Perform Overhead Throw:

-   Place yourself so that you are facing a wall or a teammate.
-   Keep your feet no wider than shoulder width apart.
-   Lift the medicine ball and hold it in position behind your head while keeping the knees slightly bent.
-   Throw the ball aggressively against the wall (or to your teammate) flexing at the hip and using your whole body to complete the movement.

6.1.3 Pullover Throw

How to Perform Pullover Throw:

- Start by lying down on the exercise ball with it placed under the low back. Keep your knees bent at a 90-degree angle.
- Keep your feet flat on the floor and make sure they are pointing forward.
- Tell your teammate to stand about 8-10 feet away from you so that you have a target to aim for (if you don't have a teammate available use a wall or something else as the target).
- Hold the medicine ball overhead with your arms fully extended.
- Contract your glutes, tuck-in your chin, and then quickly crunch forward throwing the medicine ball with all your might toward your teammate or other target.

6.1.4 Shot Put

How to Perform Shot Put:

- Place yourself sideways to the wall while keeping your knees slightly bent and your feet about shoulder width part.
- Pick up the shot and hold it in your left hand at the base of the fingers (not the palm). Your palm should be pointing toward the throwing direction.
- Position the shot under your jaw and then push it into your neck.
- Keep your eyes to the ceiling and punch the shot against the wall with maximum force, making sure to keep the elbow high at all times (lowering the elbow can cause the shot to be thrown like a baseball and run the risk of potential injury).

6.2 Lower Body Plyometric Exercises

These exercises are aimed at increasing both your speed and power. They are designed to be performed with fast movements in short amounts of time.

6.2.1 Bounding

How to Perform Bounding:

- Place hurdles in a straight line about three feet apart.
- Place yourself behind the first hurdle in a semi-squatting position.
- Start to perform high and far jumps over each of the hurdles.

6.2.2 Depth Jumps

How to Perform Depth Jumps:

- First you need to find a bench, or something similar that is no higher than 40 centimeters.
- Get up onto the bench and then drop off it slowly (do not leap off).
- Once you land on the ground, explode as intensely as possible in a vertical motion as high as you can.

6.2.3 Hurdle Jumps

How to Perform Hurdle Jumps:

- Place a bench about one yard from the first collapsible hurdle or barrier.
- Put a cone about 25 yards from the last hurdle.
- Step up onto the bench and jump off it.
- Once your feet touch the ground, squat down and jump over the first hurdle with feet together using a double arm swing. Jump over the second and third hurdles in the same way.
- Once you clear the last hurdle, perform a maximum-speed sprint to the cone and then jog back to the starting position from where you can repeat the exercise.

6.2.4 Lateral Jump to Bench/Box

How to Perform Lateral Jump to Bench/Box:

- Stand alongside a bench that is no higher than 30 centimetres.
- Jump sideways over the bench clearing it as high as possible.
- As soon as you land on the other side, jump back to your starting position. Repeat as required.

6.2.5 Ricochets

How to Perform Ricochets:

- Create a small box shape on the ground using low, solid objects, chalk or tape. The box should be about 2-foot square.
- Place yourself at any of the four sides of the box.
- Keep your feet close together and perform small jumps randomly from side to side.
- Do this for 30 seconds and then rest before repeating.

6.2.6 Single Leg Hops

How to Perform Single Leg Hops:

- Start by standing on one of your legs while keeping your knee slightly bent.
- Jump as far and as high as possible in a straight line for an agreed amount of hops.
- Do not use your arms to gain more power in your jumps.
- Once you reach the end, turn around and go back on the other leg.

6.2.7 Tuck Jumps

How to Perform Tuck Jumps:

- Place yourself in a comfortable standing position making sure your feet are no wider than shoulder width apart.
- Keep your knees slightly bent.
- Hold your hands in front of you with palms down and fingertips together at chest height.
- Dip down into a quarter-squat position and explode quickly upward. Drive the knees towards the chest (preferably touching your chest slightly).
- Jump as high as you possibly can. Raise your knees and re-extend your legs to absorb the impact through the knees (this ensures a comfortable and safe landing).

7. Speed & Agility

Once you have developed your aerobic & anaerobic levels along with a solid strength base, it is time to include some shorter and higher intensity exercise into your fitness training.

This is where speed and agility comes in.

The idea is to include movements in all directions.

This is important because on a soccer field you will not only be running in a straight line or along a set path, like an athletic runner does.

7.1 Specific Speed for Soccer

There is a big fallacy among amateur coaches regarding the speed of individual players.

I know from experience that a lot of coaches believe speed is something a player is either born with or he's not; and it's not something that can be improved on much by any kind of training, no matter how hard a player tries.

These coaches are only part right.

Of course genetics are a factor that plays a big role in an individual's ability to move quickly, just as it is with any other natural talent.

Even so, this is not the end of the road.

Speed, just like any other skill, can be improved upon with the right kind of training.

That's not to say a slow player can become a speeding bullet through a few exercises, but he can certainly become faster than he is currently, and that's something that should not be ignored.

I've practiced under special sprint trainers who were hired specifically to improve player's overall speed.

While I learned some important speed techniques from these guys, it was not possible to convert these into pure soccer speed.

The reason for this is that soccer is a multi-directional sport, which means you are not merely running up and down in straight lines.

In every game a player is required to change directions and movements every few seconds, and that's what makes this a more complex issue than just speed training; something that is perfectly fine for training other types of athletes.

I am not claiming that performing a 50 yard run at maximum speed is not an efficient exercise in soccer, because it is, but it's far from the only requirement needed for developing the speed and reaction times of a player.

In soccer terms, we see speed as:

- The ability to accelerate quickly.
- Maintain a high speed run at full power.
- The ability to act fast in different game situations.
- The ability to twist and turn quickly.
- The ability to change direction quickly.
- The ability to analyze a game situation and anticipate moves.
- The ability to control the ball at high speeds.

7.2 Mistakes to Avoid

There are certain things that you need to watch out for when developing your soccer speed.

The following points highlight the most important ones that I have learned during my soccer career:

- *Practicing with pain*: You often hear the expression in soccer, "no pain no gain" but don't take this literally, not if that pain is something more than the temporary fatigue or hurt caused by physical exertion. Never participate in training if you feel any kind of unnatural pain or discomfort. This is very important, even if you really don't want to stop, you must. Anyone who continues to exercise with an injury is just asking for problems. So if you feel any pain in any part of your body, and suspect it may be the result of an injury of some kind then, whatever you do, stop immediately, before things get even worse. Sometimes it can be hard to decide whether a muscle pain is a sign of injury or just a result of overexertion, but the golden rule is this, if in doubt, STOP!'

- *Not performing exercises correctly*: Whenever you are practicing your fitness training, you need to make sure that you are performing the exercises 100% correctly. This is really very important. By performing an exercise even slightly wrong, could result in a potential injury, even fatal, depending on the exercise being carried out. Apart from the safety aspect, performing an exercise the wrong way will also mean you won't be getting the maximum benefit for your efforts. When you don't get to see the results you have been working so hard to achieve, then the whole workout thing become nothing more than a demoralizing exercise.

- *Not preparing well*: Many soccer players, for some strange reason, believe that good preparation doesn't have that much effect on their performance. They're wrong. Anyone who wants good results has to be well prepared for every game. Good overall preparation includes eating properly, sleeping well, resting between training, drinking enough water, and not forgetting, training hard so that you're in the best shape you could possibly be in for the game ahead. Good overall preparation is fundamental for performing well in all areas of soccer.
- *Cheating on your practice*: Speed training is not something that too many soccer players relish. However, anyone who wants to become good has to take the rough with the smooth and change their outlook on this. Skipping practice simply means you are selling yourself short. If you avoid going to practice just because you can't be bothered, or because the training session is focused on speed training and you'd prefer to give that a miss, then you're on completely the wrong path. Speed training will not only help increase your performance on the field, but it will also help you to become more resistant against injuries. In other words, it is very crucial for your success as a player for a number of reasons.

7.3 Speed Exercises

The amount of repetitions and sets to perform during these exercises depends on the individual.

In many cases you will need to build yourself up before you are able to increase the number of repetitions to an impressive level for any given exercise.

However, and whenever possible, I suggest you perform at least four to five sets with 8-10 repetitions from the outset, that's if you can do so without killing yourself, figuratively speaking of course.

Obviously if you are recovering from an injury, then it's crucial that you don't push yourself too hard.

You should know what your limitations are based on the advice of your medical professional - if you're recovering from a serious injury - or the advice of your coach for a more minor injury.

Another thing to be mindful of is the importance of taking short intervals of rest between sets.

Try to keep these rests to one minute or less, except if the exercise in question suggests otherwise.

7.3.1 Speed Improver

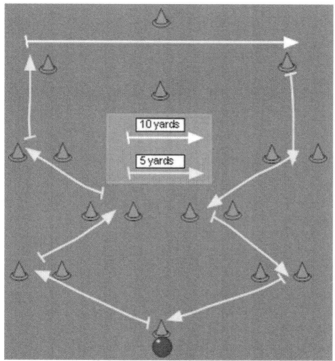

The distance marked with yellow arrows should be five yards apart and the distance indicated with the white arrow along the top should be 15 yards.

I personally like to have a half yard of space between the adjacent cones, but feel free to increase it to one yard or more if you want to.

Ok, so the way to perform this speed improver exercise is to start at the first cone, bottom center.

The idea is to sprint your way through the drill by following the path of the arrows.

You could also vary this exercise by running backwards or increasing the distance between the cones.

Note how there are numerous directional changes here, which is something that's very applicable to soccer, hence the layout of this particular exercise.

7.3.2 Stepping Strides

To set up the stepping strides you will need to place ten cones in a straight line with a distance of one yard between each.

Stand half a yard away from the first cone to the right (red point) and run the length of the cones as quickly as possible while touching the ground just once between each of the cones.

7.3.3 Number Runs

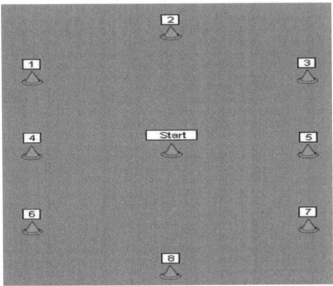

To accomplish this exercise you will need nine cones in all. Use one cone to mark the starting point.

The rest of the cones should be about 5-10 yards away from the central starting point. Each of the outer cones should be numbered from one to eight.

-   Run from the starting point to cone number one and then return to the starting position by running backwards.
-   Rest for two seconds before running to cone number two, and then return to the starting point, again by running backwards.
-   Repeat the above drill until you have been round all the eight cones. Rest for two minutes and repeat the exercise.

7.3.4 Back and Forward

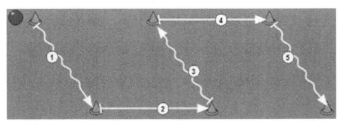

Place six cones in the same formation as the image above.

Keep a distance of about 10 yards between each cone.

Start from the cone at the top left corner and follow the illustrated path. Here is an example of how to perform this exercise:
- Run backwards
- Sprint
- Run backwards
- Sprint
- Finish by running backwards.

7.3.5 Manchester United

This drill is one of my favorite exercises when it comes to speed training.

Its chief advantage is that you can vary it in so many different ways.

Here are three variations that I use frequently, and to great effect too.

- *Variation 1*: Place five cones in a straight line with five yards between them. The sixth and last cone should be ten yards from the fifth cone. Start at the first cone and leap side to side over the cones, through the stack (using both of your legs). Once you reach the fifth cone, sprint through to the finish.

- *Variation 2*: Start at the first cone facing backwards. Count to four and then run backwards as fast as possible through the cones. Once you reach the fifth cone, turn around and perform a sprint to the last one.

- *Variation 3*: Starting at the first cone, run through the line of cones to the finish. Once you reach the last (sixth) cone, run around it and then sprint back to the first cone along the side of the other cones. Run around the first cone and then sprint to the finish cone again along the other side of the line of cones.

7.4 Agility Exercises

Complex movements on the field such as passing, dribbling, turning, etc., require high agility levels.

Your agility depends on a combination of different factors such as strength, balance, speed and coordination.

The important thing to keep in mind when working on your agility is that the exercises should mimic your movements and the specific demands of your position on the field.

For example, central fullbacks tend to use more sideways and backwards sprinting compared to other positions.

Keep in mind also that you should perform most agility drills at high speed unless stated otherwise.

This is because they are supposed to simulate your game situations. Agility training can be practiced at any time of the year.

Some parts of soccer fitness are best intended for pre-season training, but this skill is appropriate for all seasons.

You need to keep in mind that agility training should be taken seriously so try not to cheat or look for shortcuts while performing these exercises.

7.4.1 Twenty Yard Box

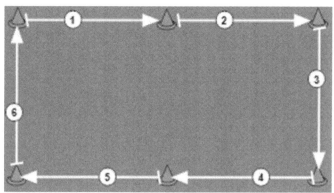

The exercise is pretty straight-forward. You start by backpedaling (running backward), then jockeying (running sideways) to the left, sprinting, and finally jockeying to the right.

Tips: Make sure you keep your ankles, knees and hips bent for the left and right jockeying movements. Try to rest for about 30-60 seconds between each circuit before repeating the exercise.

You may also vary this exercise by starting from different positions.

7.4.2 Slalom Runs

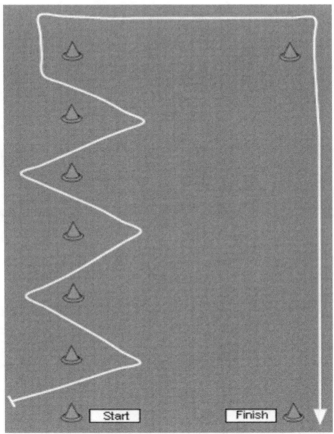

Starting at the first cone, work your way through the circuit by following the path outlined in the image.

Once you have been around the last cone, jog slowly back to the starting position, rest for 10 seconds, and then repeat the exercise.

You may vary this exercise by increasing the distances between the cones.

7.4.3 Station Runs

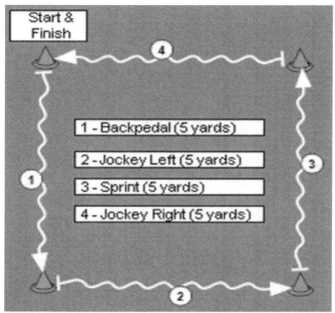

Create a rectangle with the cones placed five yards apart (see above illustration). The cone at the top left is both your start and finish point. Here is an example of how to perform the station runs:

1. Sprint to the second cone and perform 20 sit-ups as soon as you get there.
2. Now, sprint to the third cone and perform 10 push-ups.
3. Stand up and immediately sprint over to the fourth cone and perform 10 knee jumps.
4. Explode with a backward run to the fifth cone.
5. Finish with a slalom run to the sixth cone.
6. Jog back to the starting position.

7.4.4 Lateral Double

Stand with both feet together and position your body so that it's adjacent to the right side rung.

Make sure your feet are pointing forward, in the same direction you are facing.

Now perform a lateral (side) jump to the right and land into the rung with both feet.

Immediately after you touch the ground, perform another jump into the next rung.

Continue like this until you're at the end of the ladder.

Jog back to your starting position and repeat the exercise.

7.4.5 Left-Right Step Ladder

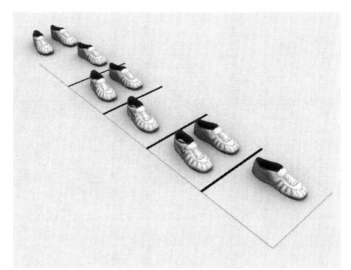

Hop into the first rung on your left foot and keep the right foot above the ground.

Hop over to the second rung only this time land with both feet together.

From the second rung, land in the third rung on your right foot while keeping your left foot above the ground.

In the next move, land in the fourth rung with both feet.

Continue with this pattern until you reach the end of the ladder.

After the last rung, jog back to your starting position and repeat the exercise.

7.4.6 In-Out Ladder

Place yourself in front of the ladder with feet close together.

Count up to four and then jump into the first rung while keeping your feet together.

Once you land on the ground, immediately jump to the second rung, landing with one foot on either side of it (see illustration above).

Jump onto the third rung, this time landing with feet together again.

Continue with this pattern until you reach the end of the ladder.

Jog back to the starting position and repeat the exercise.

8 Flexibility Training

Many soccer players and coaches believe that flexibility training is just another term for stretching.

It is actually quite a bit more than that and should be treated so.

Furthermore, flexibility training should never be performed before a competition, as part of the warmup routine.

Proper flexibility training is essential for soccer players because the more flexible you are the more you can do on the field.

This is because you can adapt your body effortlessly to meet various situations, that is, bend, stretch, twist and turn much easier than someone with a less flexible body.

Also important to note is that the more flexible you are the less prone you become to injuries, including that most common of soccer injuries, the groin strain.

Here are some of the many benefits that derive from proper flexibility training:

- *Improved Blood Flow*: With improved blood circulation your tissues will increase their elasticity, which in turn increases your performance on the soccer field.
- *Better Muscle Coordination*: The time it takes for an impulse to travel from your muscles to your brain, and back again, is called nerve-impulse velocity. By working on your flexibility you will be able to improve this function. The result of this is that your muscles groups work in a more synergistic and coordinated fashion.
- *More Flexibility*: Being more flexible will provide your muscles with an increased range of motions. This makes it easier to perform acrobatic moves during the games like the side volley or bicycle kick, as two examples.
- *Muscle Power*: You will also increase the power that each of your muscles can generate. This simply means that the muscles will be able to bend back further and also store more energy in the muscle fibers.
- *ACL (anterior cruciate ligament) Injuries*: Flexibility helps you to avoid ACL injuries in the knee. These are the most common type of knee injury, accounting for around 40% of all sports injuries. An ACL sprain or tear could keep you off the field for several months.

With so many benefits you may now be wondering why so few players actually work on their flexibility.

The simple answer is that many of them are simply unaware of the importance of flexibility training, which gives you a huge advantage.

8.1 Static, Dynamic & Passive Flexibility

It may surprise you that not so many players or even coaches, come to that, are aware of the three types of flexibility.

These flexibility types are put into two groups, namely dynamic and static.

The ones that involve motion are referred as dynamic, whereas the ones which do not are referred as static.

8.1.1 Dynamic Flexibility

Dynamic flexibly is your ability to perform a full range of motions around your joints.

With a greater range of motions in the muscles and joints, your time on the field becomes easier and more comfortable.

You will also be able to improve your overall health and become less prone to serious injury.

An example of dynamic flexibility in soccer is kicking a ball as high off the ground as possible using maximum force.

8.1.2 Static Passive Flexibility

Static passive flexibility refers to your ability to stretch an antagonist muscle (muscles which often occur in pairs) while using one of the tendons in your agonist muscle.

In soccer, this type of flexibility refers to your ability to hold a stretch when lunging for the ball or when performing a quick change in direction on the field.

One of the main benefits with this type of flexibility is that it helps to prevent muscle tearing.

8.1.3 Static Active Flexibility

Static active flexibility is your ability to assume an extended position and then maintain it while using your body weight.

One example of static active flexibility is lifting one of your legs and keeping it high without using any other 'external' support.

When playing soccer, you will use static active flexibility much less so than dynamic flexibility.

8.2 Types of Stretching

If you are new to the world of flexibility then you will probably start to feel overwhelmed when I tell you that within these three categories there are at least twice as many stretching processes.

Don't worry.

This will all make sense later on, so for now just keep on reading. So when discussing stretching we often want to separate these into either dynamic (motion) or static (motionless).

As soccer player you should focus primarily on the dynamic and static methods of stretching.

However, there are three more methods that are used which are not yet popular because they either require expensive equipment, or a willing partner who will assist you during each of your stretching sessions.

Another disadvantage with some of these other stretching techniques is that they can be dangerous.

In fact, you could injure yourself quite badly if you are not 100% certain that what you're doing is the correct approach.

8.2.1 Static

This type of stretching is performed by reaching forward to a particular point of tension and then holding the stretch.

It is recognized to be very effective for improving the flexibility of a soccer player by preventing injuries and performance enhancement.

While some studies claim that static stretching could actually be harmful, which is true when not performed as per the guidelines.

Even so, static stretching still holds its position as a very effective, safe, and popular method for increasing a soccer player's overall flexibility when, and only when, they're performed 100% properly.

Advantages

-   Low risk of injury during stretching.
-   Effective for permanent muscle lengthening.

Disadvantages

-   Less efficient for improving performance than some other types of stretching drills.
-   Doesn't increase the blood flow in muscle tissues.

8.2.2 Dynamic

Many people believe that dynamic stretching is the same as ballistic stretching (see below), but this is not so.

Ballistic stretching involves bobbing or bouncing movements aimed to stretch the muscles beyond their normal range of movement.

The American Academy of Orthopedic Surgeons advise against ballistic stretching because they say that bouncy stretching techniques can cause injury, especially when those doing them are not totally sure how to perform the exercises properly, or they don't heed the warning signs are that are telling them to stop.

Dynamic stretching, on the other hand, involves controlled movement patterns that are more specific to the requirements of soccer players.

A dynamic stretching method should be incorporated into your warm-up prior to, and right after your games and practices.

Advantages

-   Increases the temperature of your muscles.
-   Increases the blood flow to your muscles.

Disadvantages

-   Produces smaller increase in the length of your muscles.
-   Doesn't allow adequate time for neurological, or nerve adaption.

8.2.3 Ballistic

This is the oldest way of stretching and is done by performing repetitive bouncing movements.

Instead of holding your positions for a given period of time, you are actually pushing your stretch in a deliberate, yet much less controllable manner.

The moment you feel a light burning sensation you should relax before resuming with your ballistic stretching exercises.

The reason why ballistic stretching is considered dangerous is because many players simply don't know how far they should stretch.

Furthermore, if the light burning sensation doesn't come they will just keep on pushing harder and harder, which will often result in a strain injury.

Ballistic stretching is a very useful stretching exercise technique but they must be performed with knowledge and caution.

Advantages
- Mimics certain movements used in soccer.
- Can be used to help perform dynamic stretching exercises more effectively.

Disadvantages
- The risk of injury if the muscles are stretched too far.
- Inadequate adaption of muscle tissues.

8.2.4 Proprioceptive neuromuscular facilitation (PNF)

PNF stretching is a combination of static and isometric stretching methods.

To perform PNF stretching successfully you will generally need a teammate to assist with some, though not all, of these stretching drills.

This type of stretching is generally performed by involving a 10 second push phase that is followed by a 10 second relaxation phase, which is then typically repeated for an optional number of repetitions.

PNF can really produce great improvements in your overall flexibility compared to other methods of stretching.

Advantages

- Very efficient as a form of muscle rehabilitation.
- Excellent for improving your muscular strength.

Disadvantages

- Often requires a teammate to assist during certain stretches.
- Not recommended for players who are younger than 18 as their bodies are not yet fully developed.

8.2.5 Isometric

The isometric method is ideal for improving your static flexibility.

When performing isometric exercises you are applying a constant force on your muscles for about 10 seconds.

An example of isometric stretching is to rest your outstretched leg on the back of a chair (or other stable object) while you slowly try to bend the knee.

Isometric stretching is also pretty intense, which means you need to proceed with caution.

Advantages

- Improves flexibility faster than any of the other above mentioned methods of stretching.
- Improves both flexibility and muscular strength.

Disadvantages

- Not recommended for players who are younger than 18 as their bodies are not yet fully developed.
- You need a partner who can assist you during the stretching sessions.

8.3 Static Stretching Exercises

The following static stretching exercises can be used as a cooling down routine after your practices or games. It's important to breathe in a controlled manner during all of these drills.

8.3.1 Chest

How to Perform Chest:

- Clasp your hands behind your back while keeping your arms outstretched.
- Now straighten and raise your arms.
- With arms raised, bend your body forward while pushing your head close to your chest.
- Hold this position for about 15 seconds and release and then repeat as required.

8.3.2 Triceps

How to Perform Triceps:

- Place one of your hands behind the neck while keeping your elbow high in the air.
- Now, place the other hand on the elbow and pull it toward your head.
- Hold that stretch for 10-15 seconds and then relax.
- Repeat the exercise with your other arm.

8.3.3 Knees to The Chest

How to Perform Knees to The Chest

- Lie on the ground and pull your knees into your chest and maintain that position.
- Now place your hands on your hamstrings (not on the knees).
- Hold that position for 10-15 seconds and release.

8.3.4 Glute Stretch

How to Perform Glute Stretch

- Sit down on the floor keeping one of your legs bent.
- Place the opposite arm over the leg, e.g., if you have bent your right leg, place the left arm over it (see above illustration).
- The arm should be placed so that it is possible for you to use the elbow to push down on your right knee.
- Push and hold the position for 10-15 seconds and then switch to other leg.

8.3.5 Groin

How to Perform Groin

- Place yourself in a sitting position with your legs bent and soles pressed together (see above illustration).
- Slightly press your knees down toward the ground in order to stretch your groin.

8.3.6 Addcut

- Start by having both feet wide apart but be careful not to extend your stretch too much.
- Once you are in the right position, bend at one knee to shift your weight to that leg.
- Extend your arm slightly as you attempt to reach the other foot (see above illustration).

8.3.7 Single Leg Hamstring

How to Perform Single Leg Hamstring

- Start by sitting down on the ground with legs apart and your knees straight.
- Now reach toward one of your feet with both hands and hold the stretch for about 15-20 seconds, making sure to keep the knee of the stretched leg straight by tensing the quadriceps.
- The leg not being stretched can be bent so that the sole of the foot is next to your stretched thigh (optional).
- Switch to the other leg and repeat the action.

8.3.8 Quadriceps

How to Perform Quadriceps

- Stand on one leg and grab the ankle of the raised leg (not the actual ankle joint though).
- Pull your heel as close as possible to the buttocks.
- The bent knee should be in line with the supporting leg.
- Make sure to push your hips out in order to extend the stretch.
- Hold this position for 15 seconds and then repeat using the other leg.

8.3.9 Standing Calf

- Place your hands against a wall with arms outstretched.
- Extend one of your legs behind you while keeping the other leg slightly bent in order to add pressure to it.
- Once into position, make sure your back heel is completely flat on the ground.
- Hold that position for 15 seconds and then switch sides.

8.4 Dynamic Stretching

These exercises can be used as a part of your warmup routines before practice sessions and games.

Make sure you perform these exercises correctly and do not try to find shortcuts as it could result in injury.

8.4.1 Shifting Stretch

How to Perform Shifting Stretch

- Get into position (see above image) and simply shift the weight from side to side.
- Keep the motion going, don't hold the stretching position.

8.4.2 Walking Lunges

How to Perform Walking Lunges

- Put your hands behind your head and lower your body as shown in the illustration above.
- Now walk forward in a controlled motion, switching between legs as you go while maintaining the low position.

8.4.3 Bending at The Sides

How to Perform Bending at The Sides

- Place one hand by your left side and the other above your head (see above illustration).
- Reach down to the left as far as possible and then return to the upright position.
- Change to the right side and repeat the exercise.

8.4.4 Circles

How to Perform Circles

- Start by standing upright while keeping your feet no wider than shoulder width apart.
- Now, extend your arms to the sides and then pull them in across your chest.
- Hold the position for 15 sec
- Repeat the exercise for the required number of repetitions, changing the position of the arms above and below each other with each rep.

8.4.5 Carioca

How to Perform Carioca

-   Stand with your knees slightly bent, chest up, and feet no more than shoulder-width apart.
-   Step out with your right foot and then quickly step your left foot behind your right (see above illustration). Repeat this action for the required distance.

8.4.6 High Legs

- Start to walk across the field while moving your legs up high and without bending at the knee (see illustration above).
- Try to touch the top of the raised foot with the opposite hand i.e. left foot, right hand, right foot left hand, as you continue to march forward.

8.4.7 High Knees

-   Jog slowly and bring your knees up as high as possible toward the chest (see illustration above).
-   Keep your upper body upright in order to make the move easier.

9. Programs

9.1 Conditioning Program

The following is a soccer conditioning program that can be used for all prospective soccer players.

This program will increase your physical abilities and therefore help you perform at your full potential on the field.

You may not find this program particularly fun to do, but the results that you get from it will certainly make it more fun on the field, thanks to the improvements you will realize if you follow through with the program.

Honestly, during a soccer game you will stand a much higher chance of beating your opponents if you stick to this program religiously.

This program will also increase in difficulty after each week.

This shouldn't be a problem providing you haven't cheated or skimped on any parts the weeks previous.

If you have, then you will find it much harder to complete the succeeding weeks.

OK, so on that note, let's make a start.

9.1.1 Week 1

- Stretch, involving your whole body. Do this for 10 minutes.
- Jog, 10-15 minutes
- Hot foot 3 sets, 15 reps
- Knee jumps 3 sets, 15 reps
- Push-ups 4 sets, 25-30 reps
- Sit-ups 4 sets, 15-20 reps
- Various ball drills, 20 min (juggling, passing, heading, etc.)

9.1.2 Week 2

- Stretch your body for 10 minutes
- Jog, 10-15 minutes
- Hot Foot, 4 sets, 30 reps per set
- Knee jumps, 3 sets of 20 reps
- Pushups, 4 sets of 15 reps

- Sit ups, 4 sets of 30 reps
- Various ball drills, 25 min, (juggling, passing, heading, etc.)

9.1.3 Week 3

- Stretching 15 Minutes
- Jog 15 Minutes
- Sit-ups, 4 sets, 20-25 reps
- Sprints, 5 sets, 40 yard sprints at maximum speed
- Knee jumps, 3 sets, 20 reps
- Pushups, 3 sets, 20 reps
- Squat thrust, 3 sets, 20 reps
- Various ball drills, 25 min, (juggling, passing, heading, etc.)

9.1.4 Week 4

- Stretching, 10-12 Minutes
- Jogging, 15 Minutes
- Sprints, 7 sets, 40 yard sprints at maximum speed
- Pushups, 3 sets, 40 reps
- Knee jumps, 3 sets, 25 reps
- Sit ups, 3 sets, 50 reps
- Various ball drills, 30 min (juggling, passing, heading, etc.)

9.1.5 Week 5

- Stretching, 10-12 Minutes
- Jogging, 15 Minutes
- Pushups, 3 sets, 45 reps
- Sit ups, 3 sets, 50 reps
- Knee jumps, 3 sets, 25 reps
- Sprints, 10 set, 40 yards, full speed
- Various ball drills, 30 min, (juggling, passing, heading, etc.)

9.2 Weight Training Program

In order to increase your overall strength I have created a simple soccer weight training program for you.

You might want to print this out and take it with you to your local gym.

This is a very effective program for both beginners and more advanced players.

Although you might be all fired up and raring to go, please note that you should not use this program for more than three sessions per week.

Something else worth noting is that you should stop weight training exercises at least two days before a game.

During the regular soccer season you need to cut your weight training down to no more than one session, two at the absolute most, per week.

9.2.1 Legs

- Squats 3 sets, 10-12 reps per set
- Leg Extensions, 2 sets, 12-15 reps per set
- Leg Curls, 2 sets, 12-15 reps per set
- Dumbbell Lunges, 2 sets, 12-15 reps per set
- Standing Machine Calf Raises, 3 sets, 10-12 reps per set

9.2.2 Triceps

- Dips, 3 sets, 15-12 reps per set
- Dumbbell Kick-backs, 2 sets, 10-12 reps per set

9.2.3 Back

- T-bar Rows, 2 sets, 12-15 reps per set
- Pull-Ups, 2 sets, 10-12 reps per set
- Seated Dumbbell Press, 2 sets, 8-10 reps per set

9.2.4 Core

- Crunches, 3 sets. Try to do at least 50 reps per set if you can.

Ending...

My final piece of advice to you is this: If you have dreams do not give up on them even if someone you look up to says you can't do a thing.

Remember to always, always, always believe in yourself, especially when stuff doesn't seem to be going according to plan, in fact, especially when stuff doesn't seem to be going according to plan. Remember too, there cannot be any progress without some failure and setbacks along the way, there just can't be, and so be mindful of this whenever things get tough.

If you don't believe in yourself then those who you need for encouragement and support won't be able to believe in you either. Be mindful of the fact that there is only one real failure in this life of ours, and that is the failure to try.

I sincerely wish you all the very best in all your endeavors to succeed.

Mirsad Hasic

28473905R00083

Made in the USA
San Bernardino, CA
29 December 2015